N.M. LOWELL

TRUE LOVE

**The Ultimate Guide on How to The Find
the Perfect Partner, Learn the Best Tips and Advice
on How to Find and Attract Your Dream Partner**

Descrierea CIP a Bibliotecii Naționale a României
N.M. LOWELL
   TRUE LOVE. The Ultimate Guide on How to The Find the Perfect Partner, Learn the Best Tips and Advice on How to Find and Attract Your Dream Partner / N.M. Lowell – Bucharest: Editura My Ebook, 2021
   ISBN

N.M. LOWELL

TRUE LOVE

**The Ultimate Guide on How to The Find
the Perfect Partner, Learn the Best Tips and Advice
on How to Find and Attract Your Dream Partner**

My Ebook Publishing House
Bucharest, 2021

CONTENTS

The First Steps To Finding The Perfect Partner

So have you decided to take the plunge and search for your soul mate? Or you just want someone special in your life and only believe in the concept of dating? Well for each and everyone on this planet there is certainly someone who could turn out to be the special or ideal partner. The point that you need to understand is that in order to find the perfect partner you need to follow a few steps.

At the outset, you need to determine what you desire in a partner. When you are on the look out for a partner first analyze yourself, your positive and negative traits. This will help you choose a great partner. Many people have a false notion that having a relationship with someone will spice up your life and bring about happiness thereby filling the void in your day-to-day living.

This is certainly not true. Sometimes a wrong decision can actually create lot of problems in life. It is important that you

7

choose an appropriate for yourself. Before you go ahead with your search it is essential that you change and improve your existing quality of life. Try and cultivate good hobbies and habits, change your lifestyle, and have a positive attitude towards life. All this can actually benefit your relationship with your partner.

You need to be very understanding and clear about what you expect from your partner. Are you a person who gives a lot importance to a partner who is enormously good looking? Or are you looking for someone who is similarly quixotic as you? These are actually very important criteria that later forms the base of every relationship.

Today, globalization has left no time for people to get into relationships. They are not able to choose the correct partner for themselves and are finding themselves increasingly dependent on online dating sites. Websites today offer various services for people who need to learn about ways to choose a partner. As a result many people are signing up with websites in order to strike a chord between their work as well as their personal life.

What you need to understand is that however hard you try, you may not be succeed in finding a partner who is perfect in everything. After all, no one can be perfect in everything.

Relationships do mean that you need to have a positive attitude and the ability to accept your partner with his/ her imperfections.

When you begin your search for the perfect partner, start by visiting some social hang outs where you can find a large number of people. Begin your discussion by exchanging small talk about your free time pursuits, interests and other things.

Also you can spread the word among your family and friends about you being single and ready to meet prospective partners. You may never know but many-a-time strategies like these can surprise you. You may get introduced to someone that may be the perfect choice for you.

Your Quintessential Guide To Finding
The Perfect Partner

Are you on the hunt for a dream partner? People across the globe have this fixation of looking for a perfect partner in life. Well, who do you think in the world is the epitome of perfection? We all have our share of flaws. And what do people actually mean by the word a perfect partner? Are they looking out for someone who is immensely triumphant or smart, imaginative or affluent, responsive or affectionate? Phew! The list may seem to be endless unless you decide on what you actually expect from your partner.

To begin with, what you need to understand is that the moment you start looking for your partner you need to conduct a self-analysis. People have a propensity to think that having a relationship and a partner will complete their existence and even fill their world with the much needed happiness and satisfaction that they always yearned for.

This perception is not really true. The important step towards finding your dream mate could be that of you trying to enhance the quality of your life. It can be anything right from improving your appearance, your habits, your social life to your living style et al. You need to take an initiative of changing yourself as it can seriously have a charismatic effect on choosing your perfect partner.

Secondly, be very clear of what you want in your partner. Are you on a quest for a partner who is breathtakingly good looking? Or do you want your partner to have an immeasurably good social life, or someone who is equally romantic as you? Be very clear about your expectations from your partner. These are actually the fundamental questions in your search for the perfect partner. What you need to understand is that however hard you try, you may not succeed in finding a partner who is perfect in every way.

You could begin your search by visiting some social hangouts where you can find a large number of people. Try getting friendly with someone you do feel attracted. Then begin your conversation by exchanging small talk about your leisure pursuits, interests and other things. You may end up finding some similarities in the person you are talking to. Many also tend to think about having a *karmic* connection with their partners.

Another way of finding a perfect partner is through family and friends. Those that know you best may be able to make a perfect match for you.

Then comes the next big step. Once you begin liking a particular person then establish developing a relationship with him/her. Start spending ample time with your partner to get to know him or her better. You need to remember just one thing and that is to accept your partner as they are and who knows, you may spend the next valentines' day in each other's arms.

A Broader Look At Finding Your Perfect Partner

There are several singles across the globe that consider it difficult finding the perfect partner. To get a partner who shares a great bond with you as well as understands you like no one else does, is not mere luck. By taking care of few things, you can make sure that you get hold of the right person. It is very important to find the perfect partner, as the wrong one could simply make your life miserable. Only looking at small things in a person may not reveal his true personality. You need to spend some time together to understand what the person is actually like.

When you take a broader look at finding your perfect partner, you would realize there are several essential factors you need to consider. Apart from clean character and other qualities, you also need to know the concerned person's likes, dislikes, hobbies, behavior and so on. This will help you realize if you are on the same wavelength or compatible enough to stay together. If you are sure what you want from your life partner or what qualities he or she should posses, this will help you find the right partner.

In today's world, one of best ways to find a perfect partner is by logging onto a well known dating site. Dating sites help you find the right date by getting to know the person better, before you meet. You can view several profiles and choose the one that goes well with what you are looking for. There are some dating sites that allow you to compare other profiles so you can make the perfect choice. These sites also give you some good dating tips and ways to find your perfect partner so you know if you are on the right track.

As per a survey, more than half the singles have found their perfect partner through online dating sites. If you know what you are looking for in your partner, you have won the half battle and your search becomes that much shorter and well defined, making it easier to find your partner. Other than dating sites, you can also tell your friends and family as to what kind of a guy you are looking for. Use your network to meet that special someone. You can also start hanging out at popular locations and parties to see if your eyes can spot a Mr. Right.

When you come across a person that possesses all the qualities you are looking for, or if some one has made you miss you heart beat, let them know. You can be friends and invite them for a meal. By spending time together, you get a chance to know the person better. If you feel he or she is the one you would like to spend your life with, let them know over a period of time.

Revealing your feelings will let the other person know what you feel for them.

If you have made several attempts but have consistently failed, don't lose hope, as there is certainly someone waiting out there for you. Learn to search better and start enjoying dating. With every date you would get better and I am sure you would certainly come across your perfect partner.

Discreet and Personalized Ways
to Find your Perfect Partner

People want love and companionship, that's a universal fact. Irrespective of how you look, your financial status or your health, you cannot seem to survive without a partner by your side. Even those with bad experiences of broken relationships, divorces or forced separation from their partner are keen to find another hope and love in their life.

❑ Confidential Matchmaking:

Some are open about their search for a romantic angle, while others are discreet about it. Most people who have been through bad marriages, divorces and broken relationships do not want to exhibit their intentions of taking a second or third chance in their life. After all, what is life without a love companion beside you? Then there are middle-aged in their late

40's or 50's, who are embarrassed to let society know that they are looking for a prospective life partner.

Life gives everyone many chances to search for a perfect partner. But, nowadays, as we all lead busy and hectic lives, we don't seem to be able to find the time to look for a compatible partner or love mate. This is where a professional matchmaker can take charge of your search and help you find a potential mate for life. They research, counsel and judge several prospective partners that leads them to an almost perfect partner for you.

❏ Online Dating Portals:

Apart from matchmaking consultants, there are numerous online dating sites that provide confidential services for getting a date or partner for permanent relationships. Online sites are more suitable, as they offer great services for a minimum price. You can sit in the comfort of your own home and browse through the details of prospective partners.

Some online matchmaking services also provide complete social and official details of the person with a photograph. Such info helps you choose your mate in a discreet and relaxed way. You are saved from the embarrassment of going to meet him/her and asking awkward questions. You can always reject the person without meeting him/her personally. Matchmaking or matrimonial websites have become very popular in the past few years.

❑ Additional Details About Yourself:

Here are some queries asked by matchmaking consultants to help you find your life partner.

o   Are you searching for a good, long-term relationship?

o   Your educational qualifications and nature of job

o   Your current status-divorcee, single or separated

o   Your expectations from a potential partner

o   Your age and physical details

o   Details about your immediate relatives-mother, father, brother or sister

o   Your full size photograph

o   Whether you want an open or discreet service

These are just some of the questions asked by a matchmaking consultant. For an online portal, you are needed to fill up a form with basic information about yourself. Such services give you the advantage of choosing a life partner who has tangible proof about his/her background. You are thoroughly satisfied with their lifestyle and other qualities before taking them out for a date.

Many people have had a satisfying and content relationship with partners found through matchmakers or online dating sites.

Do Horoscopes Really Matter in Your Search For the Perfect Partner

The phenomenon of considering a horoscope while choosing your perfect partner may not actually apply in many situations. The important question that people often tend to stress on is the prediction of horoscopes – are they really authentic or just a gimmick played by so-called astrologers? Popularity is the added name of horoscopes and each day millions and millions of folks throw a fleeting look at their horoscopes just to know what destiny has in store for them.

Today, it has become a trend for people to question what their future will be like. Magazines, newspapers, and free astrology websites are a good source, which might give you information on your horoscope everyday. People have turned to all these sources for their daily dose of horoscopes. Human beings have this voracious longing for information about the future and what destiny has predetermined for them.

All you need to do is submit the precise time, date and place of your origin to the free astrology websites to get a correct and absolutely free daily horoscope. One thing that we should understand is that it is perfectly true to be superstitious and have a conventional way of thinking in life. But, it should not exceed the limits. Often, these truths about knowing your future can make you uneasy and you might even deter from living a normal life.

Another thing we need to recognize is that any horoscope or astrology cannot deter the future. Things destined to happen surely do and we don't possess any supernatural powers to evade them. So if you are very particular about having a horoscope match then you need to be prepared to know your future irrespective of good or bad. It is supposed that the relative location of stars have an influence over human lives. Supporters naturally give horoscopes the rank of science while disbelievers think about it as total hogwash. Hitherto, it is indeed very tricky to take no notice of the force of horoscopes in our day-to-day life. Also people who have no faith in horoscopes make a fuss by evaluating their every day horoscopes in newspapers.

Compatibility amid two individuals is time and again determined by their horoscopes. Also horoscopes enlighten us the spirit of our persona. Hence before getting married many people from different countries try and consult an astrologer in order to determine how their married life could turn out to be. In case of a new liaison or indecision about a relationship, it is a very fine idea to match horoscopes. If the two signs are well matched then the probability of the connection succeeding is very high. Horoscopes absolutely offer you the solution to understanding your partner's peculiarity and the exceptional person that your spouse is.

Horoscopes will no doubt allow understanding your partner much better, but any relationship dwells on the factor of love and adjustment that are the foremost things for a healthy relationship. Hence, we need to make sure that our lives are based more on love and not just astrological or horoscope prediction.

Does your Perfect Partner Need to Have Similar Likes and Dislike as You?

The concepts of marriage, dating, or even live in relationships, have one thing in common – adjustment. No relationship on this earth can actually survive without adjustments between the partners. Normally people have their own likes and dislikes. Two people are always poles apart from each other - be it your friend, your sibling, or even your spouse. Many people are under the false impression of finding a perfect partner for themselves. Perfect partner? So how can we actually define perfection? *'Nobody is perfect'* is a universal concept. How exactly can we expect our partners to be ideal in everything they do?

Give a thought about this – you and your partner are married. He/she is from a totally different part of the world and so are you. It could have been a head-over-heels love affair for both of you. The imperfections do not seem to be visible when

23

you are actually dating your partner. But after you tie the knot things seem to be different. You realize that you and your partner have almost diverse tastes in everything. Starting from cuisine, music, fashion sense, and almost everything on this earth. So are you the type of person who gets panicky about every circumstance in life? Or do you have the knack to tackle such a situation?

Analyze this first, before you get into any relationship. One thing that you always need to ponder about is that you and your partner will always have dissimilar tastes in almost everything. It is on you to accept things and thereby create a healthy relationship rather than fret over your partner and make your life a nightmare.

One thing that every person needs to understand is your perfect partner need not have similar likes and dislikes as you do. He/she can be totally different. It's just the way you actually accept your partner plus try and fine-tune so that both you and your partner will have a hassle free life. This can be said to be the pivotal factor for the success of any relationship.

The minute you actually appreciate your own likes and dislikes much better, envisage a partner who has comparable likes and dislikes. Again, the important factor is not to envisage somebody with precisely the identical likes and dislikes. It is almost implausible that such a human being ever exists – one thing we all need to remember is that we are all too inimitable.

If you have high considerations of your own likes and dislikes and expect that your partner should be of your own type, then it's highly difficult to find someone. You need to sketch a mental depiction of a partner you want to choose with the equal number of flaws you have in you. Then you might be successful in your search of the perfect partner. Also another strategy is to re-examine the image you have created in your mind time and again, as it will save you from painting a rosy picture of your perfect partner.

Finding Love and Your Perfect Soul Mate

Many of us feel that finding the perfect partner and soul mate is only possible in dreams and fantasies. But that's not true, there are still many of us who dream of a true soul mate and believe that one day we will meet our life partner; and like in motion pictures, really come across their dream love and live happily ever after.

Man is destined to live with his/her partner. Without their soul mate, they are verily incomplete. Neither the tranquil calmness of the mountains, nor the pristine glory of the beaches gives us comfort and warmth that a true soul mate can provide. The unconditional love, trust and faith shared between two soul mates is what life is all about. It teaches us to share, care, love and make umpteen sacrifices.

Finding your true love isn't all that hard, provided you believe in yourself and your feelings. The basic ingredients for your soul mate hunt needs you to be confident, honest, trustworthy, respectful and fairly egotistical. Be ready to face the worst, but believe in the best. Likewise assess yourself under the harsh glare of your conscience. Know your desires and needs, when it comes to settling down with a life partner-make no compromises that may prove to be disastrous later.

Don't feel that only a lucky few are worthy of a true soul mate, every single person on this Holy earth is entitled to have one or more soul mates. It is only a matter of searching in the right direction. Don't run behind tall shadows, they may disappear eventually. You may be searching all over for a true life partner, while he/she may be sitting right next to you all the time, patiently waiting for you to remove your rose colored spectacles and understand their love for you.

Having a real soul mate involves sharing things, loving unconditionally expecting nothing in return. A kind of love that a dog has for its owner or that a mother gives her child.

Be clear about your values and interests in life. There can be certain issues, which according to you is unethical or wrong. Voice your opinion to your boyfriend or current partner, at the same time give a patient hearing to all that he has in mind. Is total commitment the most important thing for you, or will you still love him when the heady romance has died away and life is very normal and dull?

Would you like to be really loved for your virtues and character, rather than being nothing but a sensual body wanted periodically for sex? Cross-examine yourself and your partner, ask these disturbing questions and put your love to real test.

We humans need a lot of love, compassion, attention, respect, acceptance and even pampering. Many of us jump into a hasty relationship only to be disheartened and heart broken. We feel anger and remorse, and ask God-why me? Relax, it is God's way of teaching us that love is a never ending search, if your soul mate is still invisible or hidden by dark clouds, let that not upset you-there are millions like you waiting and hoping for that one special person who could show them the way to paradise on earth and beyond.

Finding the Perfect Partner - Tips for the Divorcee

Having been possibly through a traumatic relationship before, you certainly don't want to be wrong the next time you find a partner. There are several divorcees who tend to again fall in the wrong trap, as they keep looking out for a shoulder to support them during the divorce.

However, as this relation may turn sour as well, you remain a lonely person not wanting to believe in love again. To help save yourself from such situations, you need to take a break after your divorce and once you are relaxed and refreshed is when you should begin your hunt for the perfect partner.

As once you did make the mistake of choosing the wrong partner, it's time to take stock of a few things before you move on to a serious commitment. Simply going by external beauty is not the right and only way of finding your perfect partner. It is human tendency to want a good-looking partner. However, that is not the ingredient for a perfect and healthy relationship. Here are few tips to help divorcees find a perfect partner.

- At the outset, when you start liking someone, do not start comparing him or her to your ex. Individuals are different and it is best to judge them separately. It is nice to be wise this time, however, comparing the two is a complete no.

- Do not get carried away by beauty or personality. Get to know the actual person behind the face before you go further with any commitments.

- Do not compromise on any factor. I understand that adjustments and compromise are important in every relation; however, compromising in the initial stage is not the right thing. When it comes to choosing a person to spend your life with, never compromise on him or her.

- Attributes and qualities of a person are more important. You need to spend some time together to check if you are compatible. You both need to share some interest and likes.

- If you are a divorcee with kids, you need to look for a person who would accept your children with open arms.

- Take each step gradually before you commit. Do not be in a hurry to find the perfect partner.

- Be true to yourself and your likings in a person. Make sure its love and not mere physical attraction.

30

- You can also write down all the qualities you are looking for in a person. This may help you find the perfect life partner. You may not come across a person who has all the qualities from your wish list, but if someone possesses majority of them, you can get going.

- To save yourself from jumping from one relation to another, you need to be careful this time to make sure you place yourself in safe hands.

- There are several dating sites for you. Look for a genuine and popular site, where you can register, view profiles, and get to know a person well before you meet them. The chances of finding true love on these dating sites are high, since a lot of genuine people are taking this way to find the perfect partner.

Keep your eyes open and learn to recognize the true colors of a person. Be alert to sense the perfect partner in a person you meet. If it takes time do not be disappointed, as there is surely someone waiting to have a partner like you who can be a perfect spouse.

Finding the Perfect Partner-Knowing
who and what you want is the Biggest Step

We all like to dream about our future, with someone who is perfect and just made for us. While some can be lucky enough to get a good deal, others learn to be satisfied with a love partner-plus all their flaws and blemishes. Well, that's life; all practical and resoundingly harsh.

But in a way it is better to be realistic and grounded that go chasing wild fantasizes. You should have the strength and character to be satisfied with what the Lord has chosen for you.

Knowing yourself is the first big step in your eternal search for a right match. Because deep within you, only you can probe and know what is ultimately the best thing for you. For example, many of us want to have a partner who can provide financial stability and security. Some of us don't really bother about a rich person; all we want is a handsome hunk that looks like a million bucks.

But, I shall always respect those people who go for true character, those wanting a love mate who is honest, truthful and down to earth; irrespective of his outer appearance or financial status. That is the partner who can have the resilience to be with you through all the hardships of life, without deserting you in stormy weather for greener pastures.

Nevertheless, it is you and your state of mind that finally decides what's good for you and what can make you really happy. I know many women who are unhappy and constantly nagging about their partners due to their average financial status, because all they care for is to have a good time at parties, clubs and on deluxe vacations.

You can find your perfect partner with some of the following practices:

❑ **Be clear and precise** - Don't be confused about what you want in life, it may never give you a second chance. Be open about your feelings to your future love mate to be on the safe side.

❑ **Be adjusting** - Life is full of compromises, if you happen to find a person remotely resembling the one that you have in your mind, be ready to compromise on trivial things and accept him/her with minor faults.

❑ **Be ready to change** - Always be ready to accept your misgivings and work on it rather than being stubborn and not wanting to change your bad habits. It is also important that the opposite person should also find all the qualities of a perfect partner in you. You have to work on any relationship to make it a grand success.

❑ **Be quick but not hasty** - Don't waste any precious time with some person who snubs you or clearly indicates that he/she has no interest in forwarding the affair. Ultimately, you will be glad that you did not have to share life with someone who does not love you truly.

❑ **Step out of your comfort zone** - Many people are hopelessly stuck in a wrong pattern, and they refuse to come out of the inner zone to the outside world of reality. That could have bad implications on your love life and your search for the perfect partner.

So the key word is to assess yourself thoroughly before running to the altar with the wrong guy.

Finding your Perfect Partner Online

Do you want to settle down in life with the perfect love mate? Do you wish to have a partner for life? Are you tired of being single and would like a companion? If these are questions that you have on your mind, then you ought to consider searching for an ideal love mate or perfect partner through the numerous online dating sites and portals. No matter which part of the world you are, the Internet can help you reach out and find a perfect match.

There is absolutely no need to climb mountains or cross the seas to find your perfect partner, all you need is online access, and presto, your dream partner could be so much closer within reach.

People have found out that apart from giving information, job opportunities and health or beauty tips, the Internet can also be used for love and romance. You get the opportunity to chat with people from different countries. You can register yourself on an online dating portal and start making innumerable friends in any part of the world. If you want, you can even narrow down your search to your own city and area.

People no longer hang out at bars, libraries, dance clubs or social gatherings for a prospective partner. Instead, they are logging on to some good genuine online dating sites for some useful details of the opposite sex. All you got to do is register on some of the top online dating sites and start browsing through their list of profiles. Online dating sites are one the easiest and hassle free ways to meet a prospective partner.

Some major advantages of online dating sites:

o   Online sites offer you all the privacy you need. You have the privilege of choosing whom you would like get introduced to.

o   You could avoid the obligation of having to meet the person till you are sure and get to know the person well.

o   Some online dating sites are free, while others ask for small nominal fees from their members.

o   With online dating, you could be in touch with many people who you feel fit your criteria and later take a call on the right one for you. All this can be done in private without the rest of them knowing your personal life.

o   Paid portals offer more security and privacy. They are more professional and committed in their approach than free dating sites.

o   Anonymity is the catchword in online dating and the fact that you are not pressurized to meet anyone until you have made up your mind.

Dating sites ask you to mention your country and place of residence, so that they can offer best services and match your profile with other similar profiles. For example, a person in China would prefer to have a partner who also lives in China. You can easily hunt for partners closer to your home.

After chatting for a while, you can slowly exchange photos and telephone numbers to progress towards the next level in romance. But, it is advisable to be cautious of devious characters that impersonate themselves and want to have fun at your expense.

Fun Dating Activities for Singles Looking
for the Perfect Partner

Dating is a great step towards finding your perfect partner. It is a natural process and as a couple, both can get involved in a lot of fun activities. There are singles that wish for a better partner and indulge in fun dating activities to get to know more about their dates

❖ **Visiting beaches**: If you live close to the beach, then you must certainly exploit such natural treasures. You can take your date to the beach for a good time and go swimming, kayaking, boating and fishing. They are popular water activities that could bring two individuals closer to each other.

❖ **Garden parks and picnic**: Take a relaxing walk with your date or enjoy a picnic with a romantic outdoor brunch or lunch. This will give you a fair idea of the culinary tastes of your partner and you can match it with your food tastes.

❖ **Museum**: An art-loving couple can hit it off at some grand museum, wherein they can enjoy each other's company amidst great artworks and sculptures. You can even boost your partner's interests in such hobbies.

❖ **Dancing**: Dance clubs have been a popular meeting place for young couples in love. It is an extremely relaxing fun activity and helps one to open up to our partners. You can just dance separately or share some intimate moments with your date.

❖ **Plays**: Some people are interested in watching theatrical plays. You can visit theater shows, music concerts, symphony or plays in your city. Such arty interests speak of a good creative and intelligent mind frame.

❖ **Wine tasting**: Tasting different kinds of wines are a swell idea. You can even get a little heady and become comfortable with your date. You can speak about the numerous types of wine and wine making.

There are many fun dating activities other than those mentioned above such as going for dinner, watching movies, going on a long drive, hiking, trekking, camping, cooking, playing lawn tennis, billiards, golf, scuba diving, poker, internet chatting or just whispering sweet nothings over the cell phone.

Going on dates gives you the unique opportunity to meet your potential life partner and get to know them better. You easily come to know whether you long to spend more time with him/her or secretly wish that your meeting session got adjourned.

Dating can be great fun and amusing if you can think of some good idea to spend sometime with your love mate. Become a little innovative and think of unique and novel ideas for dating. It will also help your potential partner come out of his/her shyness and become comfortable with you. For instance, if you have a funny side to you, you could make your partner laugh really hard and become instant friends with you.

A normal dating session can turn into a chapter of enjoyable incidents with your active and creative imagination. So, get your brains working and think up a smashing idea for the next meet with your date.

How to Attract the Perfect Partner for Life

Are you searching for true love? Do you fantasize about your dream man? Do you want to learn the art of attraction to entice your perfect partner towards you? Well, this article can give you some handy tips and guidelines for charming your way into a man's heart.

Finding a good partner can be quite an uphill task, but having him fall for your charms may be even more difficult. It is especially distressing when you see other hot females making a beeline for your handsome hunk. So it is necessary that you learn some attracting tips such as the follows:

❑ **Be Mysterious** - Men love mysteries, and more so when they get a chance to solve them. Don't reveal everything about yourself in the first meeting itself. Leave some unanswered questions, and let his curiosity get the better of him. Be secretive and out of reach.

❑ **Look Appealing** - Men like women who are hygienic and smell like pretty flowers. Be sure to do your hair and get those nails manicured. Have a great personality and confident outlook. Half the battle is already won that way.

❑ **Be Confident** - Attract a man with your confident approach. Men like confident females who demand respect. But, don't be over confident and brash. That can scare him off or make him feel defensive. Let him know about your wonderful ambitions and future plans. Men appreciate women who want to achieve success in their lives.

❑ **Be Comfortable And Real** - Don't try to put on an artificial behavior just to get the real man. It may be one of the greatest turn offs. Just try to be your own good self and let others like you for what you really are.

❑ **Be Practical** - Don't keep looking for a perfect guy, who matches exactly with your expectations. Make some healthy compromises. Be practical and don't expect your man to fall down on his knees while asking your hand, maybe he is too shy to do such filmy stuff. At the same time don't frighten or embarrass your man by going overboard to please him.

But, it is also essential that you get the right kind of attention from good men and not lecherous Romeos who are out to exploit you. Some men are just out there for some good fun and thrill at your expense. For most men, women still appear as mere objects of desire. So, be cautious-you are about to tread on thin glass in your search for the perfect partner.

Some unfortunate women are left high and dry by unscrupulous men after all the fun and frolic. Don't get entangled to these kinds of wrong men. They can only hurt and cause pain. Attract that right guy who is outwardly simple, but has a heart of gold. This fellow can make all your dreams come true with the power of his love.

But, if you happen to fall for the wrong guy, don't get dejected and start thinking that there are no more good men left in this earth. Good decent men still roam around, looking out for their ladylove. Target one and make him feel attracted like a magnet towards you.

How to Become a Good Listener
and Find The Perfect Partner

Listening plays an important role when it comes to relationships. There are quite a number of people who only hear what others say but fail to listen and hence they either land up with the wrong partner or mess up things with their perfect partner by not being able to figure out what they are saying. It is true that listening is really hard. Majority of the time we all are in a hurry to put our across point first and in this process we simply resist listening to what the other person is saying. If you are looking out for a great relationship and wish to find a perfect partner, you would need to master the art of listening, as this will help you judge a person better.

First, do not be in a hurry to look out for a partner and do not see your future spouse in every person that you meet. Try and get to know people before you would like to go on a date with them. Hanging out at popular places, parties and events will help you come across some interesting people. If you like someone, try and get to know more about them. Spend some quality time with them. Listen to every word and sentence they say. This will certainly help you understand their true colors. There is a huge difference between hearing and listening and only listening can help you see the true side of any person.

Well, how do you learn to listen? To become a better listener, you need to have great control over your mind. You need to tell yourself that you wouldn't interrupt when the other person is speaking. Learn to concentrate and don't let your mind wander. To help yourself listen better to your date, you can choose a quite place where there are not many distractions. This will help you concentrate and listen to your date better and figure out if he or she could be the perfect partner.

Ever so often we crib about having the wrong partner, however, lest we forget, it was our choice in the first place. Problems start when communication breaks down. If you would have been listening you could have understood the actual person inside. Thus, in order to find the perfect partner, listening plays an important role and one must certainly practice it.

Listening is one of the key ingredients of a successful relationship and we all need to master it. When you find partners or dates on dating sites, you need to learn to read between the lines so you can judge what kind of person you are chatting with. Later, when you speak over the phone, you can practice listening and get to know him or her better. Finding your perfect partner becomes a lot easier when you stop hearing and start listening.

Having understood the importance of listening, let's all follow it. Take a deep breath and tell yourself that from now on, you would not react, but listen. Tell yourself that you would not interrupt the other person while talking and not be in a hurry to put across your point. Listen, listen, and let your mind help you figure out your perfect partner for life.

Your Local Dance Club may Help You
Find Your Perfect Partner

We all like some love and appreciation in our lives, in fact a whole lot of it. Following our instincts makes us arrive at the doorsteps of our partner. You have to literally look up into all corners of the world for a soul mate. But, do not forget-maybe they are right next to you in your local dance club or local social event. There are numerous places where you may come across your ideal partner. But basically speaking, it's just how you create self-opportunities to meet new people in any social event, meeting or clubs.

Dance clubs are social get-togethers where you meet new faces and fresh beauties, and observe their graceful dance movements and over all personality. You can be sure that dancing is one of their favorite hobbies and if you also love to groove on the dance floor-it can be a delightful union of two dancing souls.

Gatherings like dance clubs, weddings, house warming parties, receptions, etc all are wonderful opportunities to chat up with old friends, make new friends and get acquainted with that obvious special charmer. By going regularly to such gatherings, chances of meeting your love interest get doubled. You are self-promoting yourself to interested parties, who know that you frequent such places and are a genuine person. People start trusting you and wanting to make friends with you. And that's the first likely step your potential partner may also take, towards developing a relationship with you.

Local dance clubs are more advantageous, due to the fact that mostly it is a youngsters gathering and they are all people who you know and trust. It would be very convenient to choose a good life partner from among your own neighborhood.

Some protocols to be followed in a dance club or a social gathering are as follows:

- Do not restrict your conversations to the opposite sex

- Be friendly and open to everyone, irrespective of their background, sex or color.

- You can discover like-minded people in the bargain.

- Do not be overtly friendly or talkative, this kind of approach can make people run miles away from you

- Practice your dance steps and do rehearsals at home, so that you are graceful at the club.
- Be appropriately dressed for a pleasing personality, people get automatically attracted to individuals with good personality.

Most people love to dance, especially women. Dancing is a gifted talent you can enjoy as a love couple, be it at your own house or at a dance party. Moving rhythmically on the dance floor requires technique and style-and such a person is sure to be wondrous in the bedroom also.

Moreover, you need good confidence and self esteem to dance in a party. When a man takes to the dance floor, he attracts many women, and if he manages to give right kind of attention to his lady partner-she is sure to feel romantic and comfortable in his presence.

Many partners have an instant chemistry the moment they hit the dance floors. It is a great way to search for your future partner and love mate. So, get groovy on the dance floor and woo your love interest with your magnetic moves.

You Could Find Your Perfect Partner
on a Cruise

Going on a cruise is a wonderful idea to spend the holidays. Away from the hustle and bustle of everyday life, you can relax and enjoy the calm surges of the sea. A cruise ship is often visualized as a perfect place for romantic liaisons. There are numerous cruise liners that are exclusively for single passengers who would like to team up with potential partners. You must have heard of LDS single cruise liners, the love boat cruise line, etc.

But, you shouldn't go on a cruise with a pre-conceived notion that your search for the perfect partner will end there. Go on with an open mind, to have some good fun and recreation without any romantic expectations.

All these single individuals are signed for a themed cruise liner for the simple fact that they are all spinsters or bachelors, all in their early 20's and early 40's. So there is lot of dating, romance, socializing and dances on the board. Some couples really hit it off very well with each other and develop a binding relationship that could possibly end in the altar, or you can say begin afresh!

Such LDS cruises get more popular by word of mouth, through emails and advertisements. So if you are on a hunt for a perfect partner or want to try it out with a potential partner, a cruise can be the best romantic gateways. But you have to consider certain factors before boarding a cruise ship:

❑ Take a cruise that is filled with couples or singles, not one that is filled with pesky children who get in your way.

❑ Find the age-limit for the passengers of your cruise ship. It would be advisable to board a liner with relatively younger crowd.

❑ Contact a cruise line representative regarding their policies and rules. Some cruise ships have separate zones for families and couples.

❑ Determine the size of the cruise ship. Small cozy ships are ideal for intimate and romantic couples. Bigger ships will have a large number of passengers and gaining private moments is rather doubtful.

❑ Take a cruise that heads for romantic destinations like Hawaii, Caribbean or Bahamas. All these places have good tropical weather, something very important for igniting romance and love in the air.

❑ Taking on small local cruises can be best to avoid a lot of expense in bargain for searching the right partner. Some local cruises offer good romantic dinners, dancing and overnight stays.

For more details and info about romantic themed cruises and love packages, try the Internet. You will come across hundreds of websites dedicated to serve single, couples or youngsters to a fantastic destination cruise voyage.

For example, Carnival cruise lines have themed cruise ships that offer complete fun and entertainment for money's worth. Call up your travel agent or cruise line manager for learning about such cruises where you get a chance to find your true love or experiment with a potential partner and if nothing holds ground, you can always relish the lovely moments you spent on a luxury cruise.

With cruise holidays getting more popular all over the world, it could be the most idyllic place to search for your dream partner.

Using the Law of Attraction
to Find Your Perfect Partner

We all look for a life partner at some point in life. And most of us want them to be as good as gold. But, are we aware of what exactly we are seeking in a relationship? What kind of characteristics do we expect in a partner?

Let us ask one honest question to ourselves. Do we have an attractive personality and character to attract the perfect partner in our lives? Most of us do not have an answer. We are often confused and start delving deep into our consciousness. Some feel they do have it in themselves, but mere words do not prove anything. Action always speaks louder than words.

Try to pen down a wish list full of those idealistic qualities that you are looking for in a soul mate. The following might help –

➤ My perfect partner should be very kind, generous and well to do.

➢ He should also be loyal, trustworthy and affectionate.

➢ Most important he should be ready for a good long-term relationship and love me as I am. He should accept me with all my faults and virtues.

Many of us have low self-esteem and fear that we will not be able to live up to expectations of our future partner. Such thoughts should be eliminated, in order to attract and get attracted. We should have the confidence and self esteem. We should not feel inferior or low in comparison with others. Only if you love and respect yourself, will the opposite person also love and respect you.

Let's take a look at some points to attract the perfect partner:

o Have a friendly and outgoing relation with others. Always have a smiling face rather than a grumpy long face.

o Be in the company of loving and affectionate people, their positive vibes will also rub off onto you.

o Pamper yourself; indulge in creative hobbies like writing, reading, candle making, etc.

o Always look presentable with good clothes and neat personality.

o Do not keep expectations from people, 99% they will disappoint you.

o Love one and all; do not harbor hatred or ill feelings towards anyone. These negative emotions will make you less attractive.

o Be focused and determined. Assert yourself where it is needed and have a confident approach towards life in general.

These things are easier said than done, but a little practice, a little self-assessment is all it takes to rectify yourself and your silly mistakes. For instance, if you feel angry and resentful towards someone, that person can also feel the same towards you. And if you do not control your thoughts and actions, such ill feelings will spread out and you may start getting all the more negative. It is best to remove such bad thoughts from our mind and fill it with good pleasant thoughts.

Change will be slow and gradual, but you will experience that those around you are more attracted towards you than before, all with good intentions. A good loving person is wanted by one and all.

It is a universal truth that, 'God gives us only what we deserve, not what we want.' If you are friendly, good, loving and faithful, you shall find a partner who has the same wondrous qualities.

Find perfection within your soul and God will give you a perfect mate for life!

The True Meaning of The Perfect Partner

There is no precise definition for a perfect partner except for that it could be the person who is your greatest support. We all long for a Mr. Right or Ms Right who can prove to be the perfect companion for life. Life is tough when you have to spend it all alone. As humans we do need someone to care for us, love us, and be there in times of difficulties. A perfect relationship is where both the partners compliment each other and cover up their weakness.

The saying "behind every successful man, there is a woman", is true. However, it is equally true that behind every victorious woman, there is a man. This saying is true of a perfect relationship. A perfect partner is a person who will understand your dreams, and support and help you to achieve them. He or she is your best buddy, critic, and fan. A perfect partner will know you in and out and would thus play the cards properly, for a long and lasting relationship.

With a perfect partner you never have to face stress in your relationship. As your partner understands you well, there are hardly any chances of miscommunication or misunderstandings. He or she is a person who completely trusts you and gives you the desired space you require. There is tremendous respect for each other and there is the right amount of freedom as well. When you learn to trust your partner, you automatically let them be on their own when needed, and this in turn strengthens the relationship.

A perfect partner is a person who loves you for what you are and does not try to change you. No matter what you mean to the world, you would always be treated special by your better half. A pure relationship will have no deals or list of materialist expectations. A partner who boosts your confidence when the world turns away from you is in the true sense, your better half. He or she is a person who stands by you through thick and thin.

A perfect partner is a person who acts like a guardian when needed, a friend, a teacher, and the intimate lover. They have several roles to play and pep up the relationship at every stage of life. The perfect relationship takes place when your wavelengths match, and there is compatibility and an equal amount of love for each other. To make a perfect relationship, both the partners should be willing to make the effort; only then they can be called as real soul mates.

Due to a level of understanding and never ending love, a relationship seems like a blessing when you find your perfect life partner. Catching hold of a perfect partner is not mere luck, however, if you consider a few things before committing, you are sure to find your perfect mate. Before you choose anyone, make sure you have some common interests, likes and dislikes. By spending quality time together you can understand each other well before getting closer. Join some dating sites, or start hanging out at some popular places and parties. This will certainly help you meet some interesting people and find your perfect partner.

The Top Goof Ups You Must Avoid
When Looking For Your Perfect Partner

Finding true love or the perfect partner is not easy, but not an impossible task either. Many have found real love with the right approach and attitude. Nevertheless, there are some pitfalls that you should necessarily avoid while going in for the kill!

Some of the top mistakes to be avoided while searching for your perfect partner are as follows:

❑ **Being Impatient** - For good things to happen, you have to be really patient. When you are hunting for your dream man, it will not do to be impatient. Your man may also feel that you are desperate to get him in your folds. That can make him run away from you. So be patient and give your future partner something breathing space. You are not on a racecourse, so there is no need to gallop faster, for you may actually lose the match rather than win it.

❑ **Conversing Powers** - When your partner speaks to you, do not keep on about your daily schedules or activities. Your partner needs to know the real you, not what you are doing 24 x 7. Just try to let him get a glimpse of your character and the kind of person you really are. Don't bore him about your dog's antics or how adorable your kid sister is.

❑ **Being Tense** - If you are not relaxed and comfortable, you tend to make the other person also equally uncomfortable. And no one likes to be in the company of people who make them squirm and ill at ease. The main thing is to be relaxed, and that can add a special glow to your face also.

❑ **Mr. Superman** - Most of us looking for the perfect soul mate feel that the moment one arrives in our life they would take over all our problems or that troubles may mysteriously disappear. Well, you can't be more wrong. What do you think? Is he is some kind of magical helper or Mr. Fix all? He can be a good helping hand, and that's all to it. Do not expect him to perform magic-he is no God. It would be really ironical if your partner expected the same kind of magic help from you too.

❑ **Being Impractical** - Sometimes, when you are so intensely searching for your Mr. Right, you fail to see that there are many suitable men near you. And you may actually let go that very person whom you are seeking, from right under your nose. So the key is to be practical and grounded, don't literally live in a dreamland. Keep your eyes and ears open.

You often attract those people into your life, who are alike you. They are similar to you in character and in behavior. The law of attraction wills that you draw people who are on the same level as you. If you are impatient and desperate, may be you shall attract an equally impatient and desperate partner.

So the trick is to reform yourself, probe deep within you and become a better person with each passing day.

And you shall be surprised to find that one day all your goof ups and difficulties in tracking down your perfect partner are swept away by a magical brush, and your dream person stands with extended arms to receive you.

The Myths That Keep us From Finding
The Perfect Partner

Love is a beautiful emotion, it is open and spontaneous-then why do we need to follow dictum rules for getting our dream partners?

Some of the misleading myths that keep us from finding our perfect partner:

❏ Work hard to have a great relationship:

If you are bonded with your partner by deep love and trust, there is no need to work at having a rocking relationship. That which needs the support of work is not love, but a compromise of sorts. If you have persistent quarrels and disharmonies, then maybe you have chosen the wrong partner.

❑ **Sacrifice and maintain the love quotient:**

Sacrifices and compromises are like trying to glue the broken pieces of a vase. If there are frequent want for sacrifice, then it is a subtle sign that the relation is slowly degrading, especially when it is a one sided sacrifice for the benefit of the other partner. True love calls for healthy compromises from both partners.

❑ **Trying to change partner's behavior pattern:**

Change should come from within. Haven't you heard the famous quote, which states – 'our faults and wrong behavior irritate us the most, when we see it in others.' If we are not content with the kind of person we seem to be attracting, then there is something wrong with us. We need to change ourselves and then try to assess other people.

❑ **Trying to find partner in the dream fantasy:**

Well, dreaming about your soul mate rescuing you from the bad guys or a flat tire, is just that, a dream. You ought to wake up, for it may never materialize. A middle-aged uncle or a good lady could replace the handsome hunk, in the case of a flat tire. Be grounded and practical. The more you live in fantasy, the more it will affect your real world that is full of ordinary and boring people.

❑ And they lived happily till the last breath of their life:

This is certainly dream stuff, no couple could live constantly happy or vice versa. For a balanced relationship, there must be occasional quarrels, upsets and patch ups, it adds to the real spice of life. Imagine how boring it would be, if the couple always smiled and loved each other from morning till night? Happy ever after – that should have a unique meaning to it, other than the typical storybook ending.

❑ Your need for a special someone to make you really happy:

Happiness is an emotion that happens within you, it is you who make yourself happy or sad. If you are unhappy with yourself, believe me, no other person can make you feel good.

Maybe for sometime he/she could be a comfort to your sore heart, but after sometime everything will bounce back to the same melancholy feeling. Try to be happy and contended with your own self, the world could have their turn later.

Life is a mirror; it shows us the picture that we form, not that which we want to see. It is important to treat and conduct ourselves with respect, dignity, love and confidence. And you will be surprised to find the world indulging you the same way.

The Biggest Myths About Finding
Your Perfect Partner Online

Online dating sites are a big hit and you would find half the American singles registered on popular sites, seeking their perfect match. There are successful stories to ensure that dating sites are a great way to find perfect partner by simply browsing through profiles. There are dozens of dating sites to help singles find people with the same likes, interests, and views. By reading through profiles, you can choose a person and get to know him or her better through chats before you decide to meet. This saves you from landing up with the wrong date.

Though dating sites are popular and have helped hundreds of people find their love, there are some biggest myths attached to finding your perfect partner online. There are quite a number of people who assume that it is simply not possible to find love on dating sites. The truth is it is certainly possible to find your perfect soul mate over the Internet. Of course it is different than the traditional way of finding someone at work or college, but it certainly helps you find the right person. The large number of couples who have tied knot by meeting online says it all. You certainly have a good chance of meeting your would be partner, online.

Another myth that I came across about dating sites is that, it is insecure. True that we have heard few stories of girls being duped and cheated on dating sites, however, did any of them realize that they were registered on bogus sites. Do not register yourself merely by choosing any site randomly. You need to make sure of the site's authenticity and security before you become a member. All professional and well known dating sites are secured and expect members to behave in a particular manner that will safeguard them.

Another misconception about finding perfect partner online is that only good-looking profiles or professionals in high positions find soul mates. This is not really true. I agree that one has to create an appealing profile and upload a pleasing picture to attract attention; however, that does not mean that others stand no chance of finding love. After all, a person chooses to date depending upon the interest they share and compatibility. With regards to profession, the sites are full of people from every walk of life. Right from doctors to engineers to students and truck drivers, you shall find people from every possible field. You simply need to find a person as per your needs.

There are many beginners who find dating sites to be a complicated process. Well this can be food for thought before you begin, however, it does not make sense later. If you find the right dating site, you would be amazed to know how easy it is to navigate through these sites. You need not be a computer professional to handle the site.

If you have been holding yourself from registering on dating sites merely by believing these myths, it's time you opened your eyes to the reality. Dating sites are perfect for genuine singles that log in to find love and a compatible partner. By getting to know few people, you can make a wise decision on whom to date.

Signs That You Have Found Your Soul Mate

You may be a movie bluff, if so, you might have observed that in the movies whenever the hero meets the heroine they somehow come to the instant realization that they are a made for each other pair. How we wish it to be possible in our real lives also, that we realize our true love or soul mate the moment we set our eyes on them.

As we start to walk through the valleys of life, we do hope to find our dream man or woman. But, sometimes life is cruel; although we keep meeting the potential soul mates – they all seem to break our hearts. And so the search continues.

As teenagers we keep falling in love over and over again, but as we mature we realize that we have to rise above such puppy love or infatuation. Sometimes, even though we are young and naïve, we are lucky to find our true life partner. He/she is the one who is your shoulder to unburden all your troubles, worries, joy and happiness. We rush to them for solace, for reassurance and also to simply meet and talk to them.

Some of the heartening signs of true love are as follows:

o   You are truly happy, contented and comfortable in their company

o   You do not have to pretend or put on an artificial behavior in their presence, they accept you as you are

o   You can cry your heart out or keep laughing-they do not mind it, in fact they might just join your mood swing.

o   They do not mind being chided or scolded by you; they will not turn tail and walk off on you over a major fight.

o   You can be sure that the sun or moon may change their positions, but they shall never break their promise whatsoever.

If your soul mate has even half of the qualities mentioned above, then you should really feel yourself lucky and truly blessed by God that you have such a wonderful life partner by your side.

The first and foremost thing to do before you go on a search is to find the real you-hidden behind layers of ego and artificial behavior. Who is the real you? What are your ethics and morals? How affectionate and lovable are you? Are you capable of handling true love? Are you mature enough to understand a soul mate?

Some of the other signs of meeting your soul mate are as follows:

- ❑ Having great physical attraction for each other
- ❑ Having common hobbies and interests in life
- ❑ Sharing mutual respect and understanding
- ❑ Making each other feel special and beautiful
- ❑ Being content in giving each other company, sometimes forgetting that the outside world exists

Tracking your life partner needs you to be patient. It is better to wait for a good person than tag along with someone who is unworthy of your attention. Only time can surely decide whether two souls are truly compatible and made for each other.

Till that time take life as it comes, and let nature take its own course. And if you feel like you have met your match, then quietly thank the Almighty and hope that the relationship flourishes from thereon.

Matchmakers Can Bring Together
the Perfect Partners

If you are considering a career as a matchmaker don't think twice! Matchmaking in itself has become a great industry today. The idea of matchmaking can be termed as a course of mainly introducing people for the sole purpose of dating and even for the reason of marriage.

Today matchmakers are highly professional in their business. In simple words, we can say that matchmakers are much-needed advisors who help us find the perfect partner for marriage or even dating. The main advantage of approaching a matchmaker is that they have a great network of contacts, which might help you meet the right person you were always waiting for. Matchmakers also have fairly good connections in social circles. This really helps if you are on the look out for a partner.

The basic role of a matchmaker is to bring together the perfect partners. It was mainly the part of the matchmaker to determine the compatibility and appropriateness of the two families.

Classically, matchmaking normally takes place in a society where the family unit is an exceedingly esteemed notion, and a break up is normally gravely looked down upon. The matchmaker is in charge of building an association between the two families on a peaceful and enduring basis, so the connection amid the two groups is now even more vital than the compatibility of the duo.

Also it is highly dependent on the matchmakers to verify the authenticity of the families, their background and many more. But, somehow the traditional concept of matchmaking is paving the way for more enhanced methods of finding a match. As we can see, there is a drastic rise in the number of sites on website offering matrimonial or dating services. They have many preferences from which you can choose your perfect partner without any great hindrance. As a result, the conventional way of matchmaking has taken a backseat.

Hitherto in many places in and around the world the idea of matchmakers finding a prospective bride/groom is still prevalent. People do consult these matchmakers in finding the archetypical partner for their children. Today, matchmakers need not even have their own office. They can work from home and build their contacts. Also they can post an advertisement on any website and provide suitable links to make things easier and simpler.

These days website matchmakers are turning out to be the fastest emerging world dating partners. Truly speaking these matchmaking websites have garnered huge memberships and are always improvising their sites. All you have to do is make a membership payment from the comfort of your home or office and start searching for your perfect match from a large database. All said and done, what we may agree on is that matchmakers are capable of bringing together the perfect partners.

Is the Perfect Partner in your Stars?

Are love pairs pre-determined in heaven and we humans just left with the task of searching for them on earth? Is your perfect partner a matter of destiny and luck? Do stars foretell about your life partner? Well, these are some of the baffling questions that make us probe deeper into the mysterious world of astrology and fortune readings.

Even the skeptics, who do not believe in such hocus-pocus, are curious to find out if there is any truth in astrological readings. But, many of such proclamations are based on scientific and mathematical calculations of your Zodiac sign and their stars. For example, it is believed that perfect matches for Aries are typically the Zodiac signs -Sagittarius and Leo, while Librans are a strict no-no for Aries people, according to zodiac readings.

There are many people, especially in Asian countries, who consult astrological scholars and charts to help them in their search for the perfect partner. One of the most common queries asked by eager individuals while consulting astrologers is, whether they will meet their perfect partner or real love. And whether, their current boyfriend or girlfriend is the right one for them. People think that a perfect partner will be able to erase all the imperfections in their lives.

And there are some professionals who make great money at the expense of such believers in destiny. They offer you to give you the chance of meeting your most perfect partner with the help of your DNA samples and loads of dollars. If you believe true happiness and perfect harmony can grace your life through such practices, then it can be worth trying.

When people feel that finding the right partner is a result of a methodical and astrological approach, we often wonder that can love be tamed into following a pattern. Deciding to spend your whole life with a person, who is no more than a well-planned result of star signs, can be a tall task. Love is a natural occurrence and in your heart you know whether a person is made for you or not. Being compatible is very much on the cards, when two people love each other truly. You do not need the help of an astrologer to tell you that your partner is a genuine person.

Astrology can assist you to know a person better, but it is not the deciding factor. You cannot marry a person whom you do not love, just for the sake of star compatibility. Traditional readings suggest that planets in agreeable elements assure good compatibility signs. Astrology attempts to provide a strong comparison of data and gives results based on the provided info. Understanding each other's star sign helps you to be more knowledgeable and aware. Religious beliefs should make you stronger and better as a person, they are not meant to interfere with your love life.

But the basic thing is that love knows no religion or star value, it just happens between two individuals and they share a period of life together. Searching your perfect partner in your stars is a cool idea, as long as you are not obsessed with it.

How to Turn your Dream of Finding the Perfect Partner into a Reality

Dreams often portray hidden secrets, desires fears and hopes of the sub conscious human mind. Youngsters and romantic people frequently dream of their life partner and soul mate, wishing them to materialize in real life too.

Whenever you speak one to one with your friends or colleagues, many of them voice a similar wish-that is to have an ideal romantic life partner. But most of them do not know where to begin and what to expect from their dream love mate. You should have a concrete picture in your mind. For instance, you should be able to describe the primary qualities that you are looking for in your life partner.

Some of us want intelligent and smart partners, who can share our financial burden and support the family in crisis time. Some want jovial and openhearted persons, who can make us laugh.

Some aspire for wealthy partners, who will buy expensive gifts and take us for dream vacations. Some love-struck individuals may crave for die-hard romantics, who will shower us with roses and take us for romantic candlelight dinners and say those three magic words again and again. It is important to set your goals before you start your tireless search for a romantic mate.

Relationships are not built merely by romance and sexual attractions; they also need to be built with friendship, compatibility and mutual understanding. Because; if you only go by the great physical chemistry that you share with your partner, chances are there that you may soon tire of it after some time, then there can be difference of opinion and constant quarrels. So it is best to build your relation on the basis of trust and friendship, rather than mere sex appeal.

A relationship means years of togetherness with intermingled lives and lifestyle. You make your journey together, through the ups and downs of life-you are one, supporting and holding each other-that's the kind of commitment you should share with your life partner.

Finding the correct person is just the beginning. You have to slowly build your relationship with trust, care, love, respect, affection, sacrifice, hope and faith. Even the most perfect pair could separate if they do not work at keeping their relation alive and happening. But, sadly many of us learn the lessons of life the hard way, after we have lost our loved ones due to our own negligence. While some keep jumping from one relation to another, only to find flaws with every partner and wishing to be with an old partner while having a new one.

One has to realize that true happiness comes from within us; it is not dependent on any partner. If you are a good soul, you naturally attract good people and vice versa. Dreaming about your life partner is fine, as the laws of creation involve thought process. Your dreams are those thoughts, which when merged with your active imagination and intense passion-creates a terrific universal power that can make the dreams into ultimate reality.

So dream away, if your fantasies are true-the whole universe shall help you find your perfect soul mate for this life.

How to Pick your Perfect Partner

You are single and desperately want to mingle! But, the point is where and how to meet your dream partner.

Here are some classic tips to help you find your soul mate or perfect partner:

o **Hit the party scene** - Sometimes, we keep circulating in our own comfort zone and friends circle. For a change you should attend a party where there are new interesting faces and strangers who might have come with the same intention.

o **Take a Part time Job** - If you are studying or at college, you can take up a part time job that pays you well and at the same time you could carry on your hunt for that special face. Those working with you can also be impressed with you talent and skill at the work place.

o **Chat online** - There is no need to impress youngsters about chatting sites; they are heavily into it, wonderfully chatting away 24x7. But, for all those ignorant people out there who shy away from chatting, it is best to make friends and lovers through chatting portals. One must always be a tad careful about phonies and fake characters, but it is by far a superb medium to talk and make friends for life.

Everyone has fantasies, and most of them do include a perfect partner who can sweep them off their feet (females) or snatch their hearts away (males) at the very first sight. Such things look cute on paper and on films. But, in real life only some very lucky ones get to have the ultimate partner-perfection personified.

If you have spotted your potential Mr. /Ms Right, some of the things worth mentioning are:

❑ **Similar interests** - Keep an eye and ear open to know about their interests apart from love, such as playing lawn tennis, badminton, football, watching movies, speeding away on a bike, etc.

❑ **Probe the Heart** -Looks should not be given the prime importance; it is a useful asset in the initial stages. After that it is the heart that counts. A beautiful face with a stone heart is as good as a dead partner. So, do not write off someone just because they do not look like David Beckham or Angelina Jolie.

❑ **Judge their personality** - A great stud might just get the jitters in front of your parents for sheer lack of personality and character. It is important to have a partner with a pleasing and confident personality. At the least, your love should give him/her the right confidence to assert himself. One who cannot hold an interesting conversation with you or lacks the normal sense of humor definitely holds the invisible signboard-stay away. And you better mind it.

Picking the perfect partner from a list of very good friends can be a tedious process. Some insist that they are waiting for that love at first sight to happen, whilst their future partner near them is being wasted away for no fault of theirs. So main point is-do not cling to stubborn fantasizes, they may never ever materialize.

Count you blessings if you get a good, compatible, straightforward, honest, trustworthy and confident life partner – and that's saying a lot.

Printed by Libri Plureos GmbH in Hamburg, Germany